# HISTORIC

# TO

# ABERLADY

by

## John Pringle Reid

*Author of "The Skipper's Daughters" etc.*

## Edited by Ian Malcolm

Second Edition 2006

First Published 1926

Other Works by this author

*The Skipper's Daughters*

*The Smuggler's Inn*

*Facts and Fancies in Verse and Song*

*Chiel o' the Clachan: An Aberlady Boyhood 1862-1877*

Published by Aberlady Conservation Society

ISBN
09551901-9-3
978-0-9551901-9-3

Aberlady Conservation Society
Luffness Court, Aberlady, East Lothian, Scotland, EH32 0SE

# Aberlady & Gullane
# Gas Light Co., Ltd.

\* \* \*

### Gas Works—ABERLADY
### Gas Office and Showroom—GULLANE

\* \* \*

| | |
|---|---|
| Gas Boiling Burners. | Gas Wash Boilers. |
| Gas Cookers. | Gas Fires. |
| Gas Grillers. | Gas Water Heaters |
| Gas Irons. | Gas Geysers. |

Incandescent Gas Lighting.

\* \* \*

## PARTICULARS FROM MANAGER

William Campbell

HIGH-CLASS
DECORATOR

Brighton Terrace, Gullane

Phone 36

# R. FAIRBAIRN

## General Merchant

## Stationer

## and Newsagent

Agent for

# PULLAR'S
# DYE WORKS

# Main Street
# ABERLADY

BESIDES being a place of great antiquity, Aberlady is acknowledged to be one of the prettiest villages in the east of Scotland. It is now well known to tourists, being on the main road from Edinburgh to North Berwick; and it is an ever increasingly popular holiday resort. Long before motorcars were known; and when railway facilities were few and far off, many of the well-to-do families in Haddington used to come here in the summer months for sea-bathing. Through time, the citizens of Edinburgh found it out; and a few of them used to bring their families year after year to the village for the summer holidays, until now visitors come from all parts of the country; and, in the height of the season, the accommodation is taxed to its utmost capacity.

Under the County Housing Scheme a number of houses were built at the west end of the village some years ago; but it has been found that this addition is quite inadequate to supply the demand for both furnished and unfurnished houses.

## Aberlady

UNFORTUNATELY, the beach in the immediate vicinity of Aberlady is not very suitable for bathing - even less so, indeed, than it was in the days when a row of some seven bathing-boxes stood on a sandy bank at the east of The Point, and were much taken advantage of by ladies and children. And the popularity of the Kilspindie Golf Course, which here skirts the Bay, has encroached upon the privacy of those men-folk who were in the habit of bathing from the rocks. Of course, sea bathing can still be indulged in by those who care to go a little farther. There is a nice little sandy bay at "*Green Craig*" where, with suitable tides, ladies and children can enjoy the pleasure in safety; and then, there is ample scope for all at "*Jova's*

*The Bathing Boxes*

*Neuk"*, the eastern extremity of the bay. If bathing is less indulged in here, than it used to be, it is more than balanced by the increasing popularity of the golf courses in the vicinity; and there is a variety of walks around the village, which should appeal to all who favour a quiet and interesting country ramble. In this connection, the Parish Council have provided quite a number of seats at suitable points of the more favourite walks, where the aged or the frail—or anyone else for that matter—can rest, and study nature among the trees, or watch the ever-changing sea, as it flows and ebbs in the bay.

## The Old Port

PEOPLE who know the bay now, will wonder how and where there could be any shipping traffic here; but it is a simple matter of history, that sloops and small schooners, shipped and unshipped their goods here without much trouble or fuss. The spot where they came to anchor, is practically due north from the present Kilspindie Golf Club House, Here there was a fair depth of water at high tide; and the trading vessel coming in with the tide, drew as close inshore as possible before it cast anchor; while the loading and unloading had to be done, of course, when the tide had gone back. In the later days of the shipping here, when the port was acquired by Haddington, the large building nearby, now converted into dwelling houses, was used as a storehouse for the goods shipped, or unshipped.

This house is much older than its appearance suggests, it being over three hundred years now since it was built. It was then called *"New House"*, or the *"Town of Haddington's House"*; and afterwards, when the upper flat had been converted into houses for the local fishermen, it came to be known as the *"Fishers' Houses"*; and old people about the place still give it this name.

Of late, however, it has come to be called *"Kilspindie"*, although, really, it has no claim to such a designation.

Round about the middle of last century, the large store room on the ground flat was often used for public meetings, and was the first mustering place, or drill hall, of the old Volunteers. It was here also, in the year 1859, that the centenary of the birth of Robert Burns was celebrated by the local admirers of the poet. In more recent days, when Messrs Moody and Sankey had roused a religious fervour in many places throughout the country, revival meetings were frequently held in this building. In old records it is invariably mentioned along with "the Port or Haven of Aberlady", and when made the Port of Haddington, confirmed in a charter of 1624, in the reign of James VI it is set forth – "together with the house of the said burough, situated by the said port and shore thereof, called the town of Haddington's house, with the anchorage, monies, profits, privileges, duties, and customs of a free port."

The Port of Aberlady, however, was well known on these coasts centuries before Haddington made a claim to its privileges, it being in existence in the reign of Alexander II. When the North British Railway was laid through the County, and a Station was opened at Ballencrieff for the convenience of the Haddington people, the shipping trade at the Port of Aberlady naturally declined, and, in 1845, the Burgh sold its rights of anchorage, etc., to the Earl of Wemyss. Still, for some twenty odd years afterwards one or two farmers in the district continued to use the haven for shipping potatoes, and importing manures, etc., from Leith.

Among the last of these trading vessels were the *"Perseverance"* and the *"Eliza"*, Captain Sadler of the latter living in one of the *"Fishers' Houses"*. A seafaring man in the village, called Skipper Thomson, acted as pilot for many years but one stormy night at sea, when out with his little boat, he was drowned, and never seen more. He had lost a limb in his earlier life, and his wooden leg was the only thing belonging to him that was ever found, washed up on shore; and this being handed over to his sorrowing widow, she kept it in the house beside her until her dying day. The present writer can remember the last shipload that was landed at the old haven, and that would be well over fifty years ago.

There has been considerable alteration on the coast at Aberlady Bay since these old times. The sea has made heavy inroads into the coastline around Kilspindie links, as this part is now called; while on the other side of the bay towards "*Jova's Neuk*", the drifting sand has piled up hillocks that were quite unknown to former generations. The course of the Peffer Burn has also been getting gradually shallower, and at the Point, where the ships used to anchor, the foreshore presents to the older inhabitants quite a different appearance to what it did in their own recollection. The ancient bed of the burn has been filled up, and the stream has made a new course for itself much farther from the shore than previously. Consequently, the depth of water at the one-time port has been reduced by perhaps five or six feet.

Suggestions and schemes for the reclamation of the greater part of Aberlady Bay have been brought forward from time to time, but nothing further was ever done in the matter. The bay abounds in cockles, mussels, and many other shellfish, and these were much sought after in former times, not only by the local residents but by the people of some towns in the neighbourhood. In the streets of Haddington a familiar cry at one time was "Aberlady cockles! Alive, alive, O!" And it is well remembered that on the occasion of the Haddington Spring Fast, so many of the townsfolk came to Aberlady for their supply of cockles, etc., that it was long known as the "Cockle Fast".

*Port Records 1620*

# TABLE of the Anchorage and Shore-dues of the Port of ABERLADY, as fixed by the Town Council of *Haddington* during their Pleasure, conform to their Act, dated 19th December 1769 years.

|  | Sterling. | | |
|---|---|---|---|
| For each ton of Wine or Brandy imported, | 0 | 1 | 1 |
| For each load qt. 50 cub. feet of square Logs imported, | 0 | 0 | 3 |
| Ditto of round ditto, ditto, | 0 | 0 | $2\frac{1}{2}$ |
| For every two bars of Iron imported, | 0 | 0 | $\frac{1}{2}$ |
| For each 100 Dales and Trees, one of the hundred, |  |  |  |
| For each cart-load of English goods imported, | 0 | 0 | 1 |
| For each cart-load of Foreign goods, the barrel bulk of which cannot be ascertained, | 0 | 0 | 3 |
| For each 1000 Slate or roof Tyles, and each 5 Gross of empty Bottles imported, | 0 | 0 | $3\frac{1}{2}$ |
| For each chalder of Salt exported, | 0 | 0 | $3\frac{1}{2}$ |
| N. B. A chalder of Salt consists of 96 bushels. |  |  |  |
| For each chalder of Meal, qt. 32 Bolls, imported or exported, | 0 | 0 | $3\frac{3}{2}$ |
| For each chalder of corn exported or imported, | 0 | 0 | $3\frac{2}{1}$ |
| For each cart-load of Household furniture exported or imported, and the same for each cart-load of Tar, | 0 | 0 | 1 |
| For each 100 Fish above 18 inches long, one of the hundred, |  |  |  |
| For smaller ditto, two *per* hundred, |  |  |  |
| For each barrel bulk of Goods imported or exported, | 0 | 0 | $\frac{1}{4}$ |
| For the anchorage of each Ship of 300 tons and upwards, | 0 | 2 | 6 |
| 150 to 300, | 0 | 1 | 3 |
| 80 to 150, | 0 | 0 | 9 |
| 50 to 80, | 0 | 0 | 6 |
|  | 0 | 0 | 4 |
| Ferry boats, | 0 | 0 | 2 |
| Small ditto, | 0 | 0 | 1 |

All goods livered out of one Vessel into another, pay only half shore-dues.

For every ton of Coals imported or exported, 0 0 $\frac{1}{4}$

N. B All residing Burgesses within the Town of Haddington, pay only the half of the above dues, and nothing for Coal.

*Port Dues 1769*

# TABLE

OF THE

## horage and Shore Dues

OF THE

### PORT OF ABERLADY,

As fixed by the Town Council of HADDINGTON during their pleasure,
conform to their Act, dated 18th January, 1831.

|  | s. | d. |
|---|---|---|
| For each Ton of Wine or Brandy imported, | 1 | 1 |
| For each load, qt. 50 cubic feet, of square Logs imported, | 0 | 2 |
| For ditto ditto of Round Ditto ditto | 0 | 2 |
| For every Six Bars of Iron imported, | 0 | 0½ |
| For each 100 Deals and Trees one of the hundred. | | |
| For each Cart-load of goods imported, | 0 | 1 |
| For each Cart-load of Foreign Goods, the Barrel Bulk of which cannot be ascertained, | 0 | 3 |
| For each One Thousand Slates, Roof and Drain or other Tiles, | 0 | 3 |
| For each Chalder of Salt exported, | 0 | 3 |
| N. B.—A Chalder of Salt consists of 96 Bushels imperial, | | |
| For each Chalder of Meal, qt. 32 Bolls or 320 Stones imperial imported or exported, | 0 | 3 |
| For each Chalder of Corn, or 96 Bushels imperial imported or exported, | 0 | 3 |
| For each 100 Fish above 18 inches long, One of the Hundred, | | |
| For smaller Ditto, Two per Hundred. | | |
| For each Barrel-Bulk of Goods, exported or imported, | 0 | 5—12 |
| For each Ton of Potatoes, Carrots, Rape, Linseed Cake, or Dust, and Bones for Manure, | 0 | 1 |
| For each Ton of Turnips, Manure, Coals, Stones, or Bricks, imported or exported, | 0 | 0½ |
| For the Anchorage of each Ship, of 300 Tons and upwards, | 2 | 6 |
| ————————— 150 to 300 | 1 | 3 |
| ————————— 80 to 150 | 0 | 9 |
| ————————— 50 to 80 | 0 | 6 |
| ————————— 20 to 50 | 0 | 4 |
| ————————— Ferry Boats, | 0 | 2 |
| ————————— Small Ditto, | 0 | 1 |

All Goods delivered out of One Vessel into another pay only Half
Shore Dues.

N. B.—All Burgesses residing within the Town of HADDINGTON, pay
only the Half of the above Dues, and nothing for Coals.

*Port Dues 1831*

8

Notice of Sale 1844


## Development in Travelling Facilities

BEFORE railway travelling was available, Aberlady was a stopping place for the Stage Coach that plied between Edinburgh and North Berwick, and those who could not afford to travel in this way could usually get a lift on the carrier's cart. Dawson of Aberlady and Brotherstone of Gullane ("John the Carrier") were widely and long known as trusty carriers. They journeyed regularly to Edinburgh, Leith, and Haddington providing the merchants, and others, with a means of getting their supplies. The carriers' business was considered one of much importance in those days, and was a fairly good paying concern. When the main line of the North British Railway was opened, Longniddry Station was the nearest to the village, and a Gullane 'bus was started by the hotel proprietor there (Mr Stevens), which also served Aberlady, picking up and letting down passengers as it passed.

Through time Aberlady initiated a service of its own, and for many years the two ran regularly twice a day to Longniddry. Passengers were not always plentiful, but the means of travel was there if wanted, and it was a convenience long appreciated. No doubt in stormy weather some hardships had to be endured, but in decent weather the drive was a real pleasure. Many, of course, of the younger people especially, were in the habit of walking the distance, which, after all, was only three miles, and walking was a commoner accomplishment then. Besides being accustomed to going to Longniddry to get a railway connection, many of the villagers would often tramp over to Haddington for anything they could not get locally. Indeed, it is on record that some people both of Aberlady and Gullane thought it nothing extraordinary to walk to Edinburgh or Leith on a Sunday to attend church there, and come home the same way.

When the Aberlady and Gullane branch railway line was opened, some thirty years ago, the trade of the 'busmen received a severe blow, and through time had to be given up. Some of the villagers clung to the old order of things for a time, but the claims made by the new and more convenient means of travel eventually carried the day. The last 'busman who kept up the connection by road to Longniddry Station was John Pincott, who was a noted expert at packing a crowd into his two-horse brake. Now that Aberlady has a station of its own, railway passengers are set down within three-quarters of a mile from the village. The station has advanced considerably in importance, business having increased to an appreciable extent since its opening; while, by road, the motor traffic through the village is now enormous, especially in the holiday months.

At time of writing it seems as if the travelling public are about to revert to the use of the road again, a regular motor 'bus service having now been established, and largely patronised.

Suppose the visitor to Aberlady comes by rail, he enters the Parish before he leaves the main line at a picturesque spot where any observant eye will notice, on the north side of the railway, an old ruin and a large dove-cot built of solid masonry, as they usually were, to stand the test of time. This is Redhouse Castle and Gardens, a favourite subject of local and other artists. Here at practically any season there is, to the artistic taste, a great temptation to depict a bit of the scene on canvas. The old ruin and gardens have an imposing situation as seen from the railway, with a gentle slope to the south, and nicely sheltered by surrounding trees.

"*Redhouse*" has been a ruin for many generations, and is now the property of the Earl of Wemyss. This desirable little estate was held in the fifteenth century by a family of the name of Laing, one of whom was High Chancellor of Scotland in 1483. Later it came into the hands of a branch of the Earl of Haddington's family, the last of whom lost both life and lands for having supported the cause of Prince Charlie in 1745. The Finlayson family has now been tenant for some generations, and has well preserved the beauties and antiquities of the place. In a newspaper dated 1786 there is the following advertisement: -

"The farm of Redhouse to sublet for nine years. There is an exceedingly good dwelling house, commanding a most extensive and beautiful prospect. There is also a garden and three dovecots, all well stocked. Having a command of water, and more offices than required, a soap or starch works, a distillery or a brewery could be erected at a small cost, the latter being much wanted in this part of the country".

None of these suggested works were ever erected, so far as I can learn, but there was a hostelry nearby at one time called the "*Chance Inn*". No vestige of it now remains, although the spot where it stood still goes by that name. The public road from

*Redhouse Castle*

Longniddry to Drem passes quite close to Redhouse, from which it can also be viewed to advantage.

After the train has entered upon the branch line to Gullane, passengers may observe, away towards the east, another ruin having a fine situation. This is Ballencrieff House, not nearly so old as Redhouse, but of much interest. It was the East Lothian seat at one time of the Murrays of Elibank, and the present Lord Elibank, now a very old man, was born there. These old walls, rising to a fair height, and of immense thickness, as was the rule in the period in which they were built, with a series of vaulted cellars in the basement, have little claim to anything in the way of ornate architecture, but were of such a substantial nature that they might have remained in occupation for many generations but for a most unfortunate accident. In the year 1868 fire broke out in this mansion-house, and the old housekeeper who occupied it at the time, and who apparently did not realise the danger of such an outbreak, tried to put it out with pails of water, with the result that it was burnt to the ground. Only the walls now remain, the happy home of innumerable starlings and jackdaws, as well as the creamy barn owl, with the soft silent wings, and the eerie midnight cry. The view from the upper windows of this house when in occupation must have been very fine. The situation was well chosen for a commanding outlook upon a wide and varied range of scenery. A park with many majestic trees surrounded the mansion-house, and the gardens, run on commercial lines, have long been noted for the quality of their produce. These gardens, with the old park and ruins attached, were sold a few years ago to the tenant, Mr P. McLaren.

The farm of Ballencrieff, one of the largest and best in East Lothian, and which had belonged to the Elibank family for three or four hundred years, was broken up into small holdings some twelve years ago. Since then the other farms on this estate have also been sold, so that Lord Elibank who was, not so very long ago, the largest landowner in the Parish has now, unfortunately, no ties of proprietorship whatever.

As far back as the twelfth century a hospital was founded at Ballencrieff, and dedicated to St Cuthbert. Some remains of it still stand, and may be seen at the west end of the gardens, although in recent times they have been used for quite different purposes. It is still known, however, as "*St Cuthbert's*".

## The Approach to Aberlady and the Parish Church

SUPPOSE, now, that the visitor comes to Aberlady by road from the west, he will enter the boundary of the parish immediately after he passes the recently formed Longniddry Golf Course. Here on the South side the road skirts the Gosford policies; and on the north one cannot fail to recognise one of the finest stretches of the Firth of Forth. There is a fine view of the Fife coast, if it is a clear day, from about Elie in the east to Burntisland in the west; while the uplands are easily distinguished - Largo Law, and the Lomonds, with the lofty Ochils closing in the view to the north-west. Along the shore is a narrow stretch of fine attractive links, with patches of sand dunes, and a boulder-strewn beach, knowes covered with green bracken, clumps of dog-roses and sweet briars, and large beds of cowslips, or cranesbills, according to the season. Then, cutting slightly inland through a sheltering wood, and along a fine level road girded on each side by a strip of beautiful bushes and trees, there comes into view one of the most imposing entrances to any village in the country.

Before you is the Parish Church, while on one side you pass the Bowling Green, with its neat little pavilion; and, adjoining the Green is the War Memorial and the Memorial to the late Lady Wemyss - an old Venetian Fountain. The piece of ground around these has been tastefully laid out; and seats are now provided for the use of visitors. The lines quoted on one of these seats should arrest the attention: -

> "The scent of a flower for pardon,
> the song of a bird for mirth,
> we are nearer God's heart in a garden,
> than anywhere else on earth."

Looking beyond, over the intervening fields, away to the north, there is a beautiful open prospect, with the wide bosom of the Firth reflecting the many coloured clouds, as they settle down to a rosy sunset. Then, just before you reach the churchyard gate, you will notice a rather uncommon erection of masonry, locally known as the *"Loupin'-on Stane"*. There are not many such in the country, or in any country, and it must be of somewhat ancient date. It was used in bygone times by the ladies coming out of church to mount their horses; for, no doubt, they came from fairly long distances in those days, and their ponies would be the principal means of getting about.

Now we have reached the Auld Kirk, and it is well worthy of a good look, and reverent inspection. One can see at once that the building is not all of one date. The tower is the oldest part, and dates back to the twelfth or fourteenth century. Whether the church suffered destruction in Reformation times, I cannot say, but a considerable time after that upheaval, the body of the church was "renovated" but not, by any means, improved. This eighteenth century building was similar to many others erected at the time throughout the country - a very plain and unattractive place of worship. Indeed, it had quite justly, perhaps, been called ugly, but before its days were numbered it had become to many dear, if not beautiful, through long years of sacred and cherished associations.

Many still living will remember its appearance, both inside and outside. It is easier recalling its inside characteristics. It was not over-well lit, and the pews being painted a very dark colour, it presented a very dingy appearance. There were galleries at the sides, and at the back, and these retained the old square box style of family pews, occupied generally by the landed proprietors, and tenant farmers. This church in its palmy days of last century was long associated with the precentorship of Sandy Paterson and Tammy Bird.

Among men of note who ministered to the people in this church may be mentioned the Rev. John Gray, (Episcopal) a native of Haddington, who left his valuable library to that town, along with a sum of money for its upkeep. He died in 1717, and his bequest was highly esteemed by his native town, and has been carefully guarded by the authorities thereof. It still exists, known as the Town's Library, and contains many of the rare and valuable volumes originally presented by Mr. Gray. Dr. Neil Roy, at the close of the eighteenth century, was also a clergyman of some eminence. The last minister of the real old school, connected with the old church, was the Rev. John Smith, whose charge lasted from 1819 to 1861. Many stories still hover around the place regarding the quaint manners and personal characteristics of Mr Smith. He was the last occupant of the old manse, an unpretentious building standing near the south east corner of the churchyard. Mr Smith was an old batchelor, and did not bother the heritors about any improvements, being content to leave things as they were.

His successor, however, the Rev. J. W. Tait, who came to Aberlady in 1862, proceeded to make considerable improvements. It was for him that the present commodious and finely situated manse was built; the grounds also, being beautifully lay out at that time. Mr Tait, whose uncle was the

*Auld Manse*

*Loupin-on-Stane*

*Auld Kirk*

Archbishop of Canterbury, had always a leaning towards a more ritualistic form of worship than was common in the Scottish church then, and he left Aberlady to become an Episcopalian clergyman. He left the country not long after, taking up an influential charge in Rome, where, after a lengthy ministry, he died. The Rev. John Hart followed Mr. Tait, and it was during his incumbency that the present beautiful church was built.

About the year 1886, the late Lord Wemyss completely renovated the old church. It was a real renovation this time, a restoration and improvement upon the fair proportions of the pre-reformation building. The whole of this extensive restoring and re-building was done at Lord Wemyss' own expense. Being a man of much artistic taste, and sparing neither trouble nor means, it was made one of the most beautiful churches in the country. The whole of the inside was re-fashioned to good effect, making the once dull commonplace surroundings a very masterpiece of architectural taste and skill. The main walls were lowered, new aisles were built to the south side of the church, and the old aisles at the north side were once more incorporated in the building. These latter had been excluded from the body of the church by the eighteenth century builders, as being, no donbt, too ornate for their reforming turn of mind, and were set-aside as a shed to house the gravedigger's tools. One cannot view the particularly fine window at the west side of the north aisle without deploring the tendency to destroy the beautiful in ecclesiastical architecture that characterised those Reformation times. Thanks are consequently due to Lord Wemyss for having preserved this ancient part of Aberlady church, and it may be noticed that the whole scheme of the building conforms to that pre-Reformation design.

A feature of the church is the series of beautifully stained glass memorial windows, and a finer set will not easily be found anywhere. There is also a notable piece of sculpture housed here in the form of a marble effigy of the Countess of Wemyss, mother of the Earl who restored the church. It was originally exhibited at the Edinburgh Exhibition of 1887, and drew much attention and admiration for the wonderful beauty of its workmanship. Various interesting memorials will also be found adorning the inside walls, and these include tablets, etc., to members of the Wemyss, Hope, and Elibank families. The present minister of the Parish, the Rev. Thomas Caldwell, B.D., is always pleased and proud to admit interested visitors to view the church.

Around the church lies the peaceful churchyard, where "the rude forefathers of the village sleep", and to those of an antiquarian turn of mind, as well as to those who would poke into the history of the place, and the habits of the people, it is a storehouse of great interest and information. There are many very ancient tombstones to be seen here, upon the examination and study of which, hours might be spent, and volumes written.

## The Village and its Old-Time Features

AND now we must have a look at the village of Aberlady itself. The inhabitants have long been in the habit of calling it, with some pride and tenderness in many cases, *"the village"*, but it was really called a town at one time, as ancient records show. It consists, as statistical accounts tell us, "of one long street of a good appearance, and a lane running down to the sea"; yes, and nowadays, a few other odds and ends too.

Here one feels he is in a truly rural village, with the houses all jumbled about, interspersed with trees, and flowerpots, and a variety of architectural features, which all combine to make it so pleasing to the eye. If you approach it from the west, you will pass, just after you enter the street, two of the largest houses in the district - the Manse on the north side, and the Lodge on the south side. Both, unfortunately, are largely shut in from the public gaze. The Manse has already been mentioned; and the Lodge is an exceedingly handsome building, now the property of Miss Punton, a member of a family long and honourably connected with the locality. It was the home for many years of the Traill family, one of whom, Mr. Robert Traill, was a noted florist in his day, and the raiser of a number of varieties of auriculas, which even in recent years, have been seen exhibited on show tables. The last survivor of the family was Miss Anne Traill, who was for many years one of the most familiar figures in the village. She was of a charitable nature, and greatly interested herself in educational matters; her bequests, in the shape of bursaries, etc., to the county, as well as local, being well known. She was also the founder of the village library.

In the middle of the village is the Cross, very old and very plain, consisting of a square pyramid of stone steps surmounted by a pillar. It looks unfinished, and is said to have had, at one time, some emblem, ball or ornamentation on the top. Of this there seems to be no certainty; but the only thing the writer ever saw on it was one of his young school companions, who, in a fit of bravado, climbed the pillar and stood on one foot on the top, to the delight and amazement of all the schule. It must be of very ancient date, probably of about the same as the *"Loupin'-on-Stane"*, and very likely used for the same purpose that is, standing on the steps to mount the pony or cart. At all events, its original position was in the middle of the street, and if any markets were then held, it would be in this vicinity.

There are a number of old houses in the village, some of them dating from the seventeenth century. Adjoining the school on the west side is a good-sized modern-looking dwelling; but its main walls belong to a bygone time, although now dressed in a new coat. The school itself, although still presenting quite a fresh appearance, is nearly sixty years old. Opposite the Golf Hotel is one of the oldest houses now standing; and seen at certain angles, it is a very picturesque building. It was for many years around the middle of last century, the headquarters of Dawson, the carrier. A good number of the smaller houses at that time had thatched roofs, and a few of these survived for some time longer.

At the east end of the village, at the *"Braeheids"*, stands a large house of much interest, occupied in recent times by the tenants of the gardens there. It possesses some quaint architectural features in its interior construction, and must have been a house of some importance in old times. In the eighteenth century it belonged to a family of the name of Burn, the last of whom was Captain Peter Burn, R.N., who served under Lord Nelson, and was present at the bombardment of Copenhagen in 1801. The late Mr. Peter Burn Swinton, so well known throughout East Lothian, was a descendent of this family.

Near the foot of *"The Wynd"* stands another interesting old building, generally known as the *"Old Ship"*, from its having a ship in full sail cut out in stone on the front wall. The house was renovated in recent times by the present proprietor, Mr. T. P. Waggot. Its most famous owner and occupier was Captain Smith, a retired seafaring man, who was widely renowned for his strength, and had also some dealings in contraband, when that business was at its height. The following epitaph on his tombstone keeps green the memory of his unusual physical powers: -

"Here lies Jamie Smith,
wham death slew for a' his pith,
the starkest man in Aberlady –
God prepare an' mak' us ready."

This building is the central scene in the local story *"The Skipper's Daughters"*.

Further north in the same line, indeed the last houses in this direction, and nearest to the sea, was the property belonging to the old Aberlady family of Maule. It consisted of a row of small houses called *"Mussel Raw"*, which has long ago disappeared. This is the site of the nicely situated *"Linksfield"*, built by the late Mr. J. M. Brydon, Edinburgh, and long occupied by that family. Later, it came into the hands of the late Mr. Tennant Ronald, who further improved and extended it. Adjoining, between this and the *"Old Ship"* is the old *"Cockle Square"*, the houses in which, have been greatly improved in recent years, and now designated *"The Square"*. On the south side of this cul-de-sac was the Duncanson's property, also much improved since the old days. The last male representative of this family, Tammy Duncanson, was a noted character in his day, having the reputation of being a miser. He presented a striking and picturesque figure, as he went, as regular as clockwork, to the church on Sundays, dressed in what people said was his grandfather's coat, a green swallow-tail with brass buttons, knee breeches, and silk stockings. He was employed in Gosford grounds, and was a man of good education, and character, and a Latin scholar. He left behind him a large pile of manuscripts, mostly on botanical and kindred subjects, written in the most perfect copperplate writing anyone could wish to see. There was also among his papers a plan of Gosford ponds, as they were originally laid out. His weird, old, bent figure, in his later days, his silent ways (for he scarcely took any notice of anybody), and his reputed characteristic, made him an object of awe to the children of the time. He was the one and only miser known in the district, although the spendthrifts - men who squandered their means, or their earnings - might have been counted by the dozen.

*"The Wynd"* itself, facetiously dubbed *"Quality Street"* by the wags of old, is not the show place of the village, being of quite an unlovely appearance; but it is closely associated with the stirring times of the past. It was often the scene of much hilarity, and sometimes of bloodshed. One of the earliest sights revealed to the writer's wondering gaze when a child, was looking out of a window which had a full view of *"The Wynd"*, as the evening shadows fell on a beautiful harvest day, and seeing two contentious bands of Irishmen having a regular fierce battle. They were stripped to the shirt, those whose shirts had not been torn from them, and blows and kicks were profusely administered to one another; some of the contestants bleeding freely from the nose and mouth, and others lying prostrate on the ground and shouting in pain and fury. What it was all about none of the villagers seemed to know—perhaps it was for fun; but to the infant mind it was a terrible revelation of the strife of the world into which he had been ushered; and sometimes the thought comes back to him still, like a wild dream out of the long bye-gone.

In the height of the smuggling days it must have been the scene of many exciting incidents. One old doggerel verse has it: -

> "Rin doon the Wynd, Willie Crunk,
> Flee quick this nicht, John Arnot,
> The Dutchman's; lichts are showin',
> Just arrived direct frae Flushing,
> The coast is clear, get oot the ankers,
> And cheat a' the preventive Jankers!"

The property running down the east side of *"The Wynd"* to the bottom, belonged to the Christisons, one of whom, Tammy Christison, was widely known in his day. He was a stonemason, and it was he who did all the wonderful grotto work throughout the policies of Gosford, much of which remains to this day to testify to his skill. He latterly got into trouble and expense, by erecting a structure on the Sea-Green, which, after a lawsuit, he had to remove.

Near the middle of *"The Wynd"* on the east side, was Sandy Forest's public house, a flourishing howff round about the middle of last century, where many noted characters of the district foregathered. The past generation had many tales to tell of the ongoings there, and the well-known frequenters of Sandy Forest's Howff. On the other side of the street were the Malt Barns, where for many years, a good business was done. This was originally owned by Mr. Dunlop, a Haddington distiller, who imported a large quantity of barley through the port. These maltings, including those at the east end of the village as well, were afterwards taken over by Mr. P. Punton, Aberlady Mains, and latterly by Mr. F. Punton, who sent the produce to his Red Lion Brewery, at Winchester. The making of malt was discontinued here about thirty years ago.

Adjoining the Malt Barns, strangely enough, was the former U.P. Church, originally called the *"Meeting House"*, where the Rev. Watt ministered for a time. It was mostly associated with the Rev. David Nicol, who was a strong denouncer of heretical thought, and popish rituals, and who declined to introduce the hymn-book into his services, holding that the psalms were quite sufficient for all purposes. The last pastor here was the Rev. A. C. Wedderspoon, who was largely instrumental in raising the funds to build the new U.F. Church and manse. Mr. Wedderspoon emigrated to New Zealand, where he still resides.

On the other side of the public road at the foot of the Wynd, was the property of the Dickensons, another respected old Aberlady family; and further east was the *"Slate-Ha'"*, where stood the square doo-cot, a landmark remembered only by the older natives.

The following letter appeared in the *Haddingtonshire Courier* on 5 August, 1892:

### A PLEA FROM ABERLADY DOVECOT

"Sir, - I am one of the oldest pieces of masonry in the village of Aberlady. Along with the Loupin' on Stane and the Cross, I am pointed out as a relic of antiquity of which the village is proud. Besides my claim to consideration as a relic of long past days, I have also that of being a fine example of my particular style of dovecot architecture. Judge then of my consternation on hearing that it is proposed to remove me from the place on the Luffness road I have so long adorned. Surely, the kind lord of the manor who takes so much interest in the improvement of the green in front of me will not consent to the removal of one of the many attractions. – I am &c,

THE OLD DOVECOT

Aberlady, August 2, 1892"

*The old Square Doo-Cot, where stands "Slate-Ha'" today*

*"The Wynd", dubbed "Quality Street" and the location of Sandy Forest's Howff*

# Gosford.

VISITORS to Aberlady invariably want to see Gosford among the first places of interest; and they are usually allowed into the Grounds on Saturday afternoons and Sundays; while a permit can, at convenient times, be obtained from the Estate Office to view the inside of the House. This magnificent structure was finished, at great expense, by the late Lord Wemyss in the year 1887. It had been commenced and nearly finished by a former Lord Wemyss, in 1800, but was never occupied, it being discovered that the walls were damp, owing, it was suspected, to the use of stone or sand from the seashore in its construction. Nevertheless, the central portion of the present building is that erected in 1880.

Those who have the fortune to get a private view of the house will find much to interest and admire therein, the marble hall, the valuable collection of paintings by old masters, the china, and other curios, etc., are all a treat to see, and give the visitor a rich reward for his visit. The paintings themselves have long been famed as one of the finest private collections in the country, and in this spacious new mansion, they are seen to good advantage. Fine taste and discrimination have been shown, and large sums must have been expended, in the collecting of these works of art, which embrace some of the best examples of the various masters represented.

The privilege of walking in the Grounds, on the days mentioned, is one that is greatly appreciated, and should be carefully guarded against abuse, for here one is in a very paradise of beauty. The spacious parks, the shady, finely diversified woods, with a rippling stream stealing through their densest solitudes, or tumbling over a sudden waterfall, the cool depths of the series of ponds, with their happy waterfowl, and broad beds of waterlilies, and the many rare arboricultural specimens found in the shrubberies, are all worth going a long way to see.

No doubt one requires to know the policies fairly well to be able to get at the many beauty-spots, or the objects of special interest; but if one comes across them unawares, the delight will probably be all the more.

Gosford, and its lands in the parish, belonged at one time to the Earl of Portmore, a family which seems to have become extinct; and it is said that James V was a frequent visitor here, ostensibly for golfing and archery, but really for the company of its ladies. Viewed from the Calton Hill, Edinburgh, looking east, Gosford House is a conspicuous object in the landscape, and also from many points of vantage on the road from the capital. As one comes nearer, it seems to become more hidden by trees and the boundary wall. It possesses two very fine entrance gates, one near Longniddry station, and the other facing north, about a mile from Aberlady village.

What remains of the old house - the home of many generations of its noble family - is now a picturesque ruin. It was of no small importance in its day, however, and it was here that the celebrated collection of paintings was originally housed. Adjoining this are the fine old stables, a reminder of the time when many magnificent horses were kept here, and of the Lord Wemyss of two generations back, who was a noted figure on the hunting field. He continued to take a canter on his favourite hunter till a short time before his death, when he was a good long way over eighty years of age. It was the late Earl of Wemyss, however, who, besides erecting the palatial new mansion, brought fame to the place through his own personality, and the many notable people he brought as visitors to Gosford.

# Luffness

AS Gosford estate occupies the greater portion of the parish on its western side, so Luffness estate occupies a similar position on the eastern side, and the lands of both are of much value, and well-wooded. Luffness House is not of the magnificent standard of Gosford, but it is of more ancient date, and has many connections with some of the most stirring events of Scottish history. Whenever the visitor comes in sight of it, with its massive old walls and lofty gables, a bit of the old stronghold here, and a bit of the baronial style there, set amidst a group of trees of many centuries growth, he at once feels that here he has before him the scene and soul of old-world romance.

Its records date back to the twelfth century, when it is said to have come into the hands of an English merchant named Lundy. Sometime later, the "lands and port of Luffenach", which was its original Gaelic name, came into the possession of David de Lindsay, the ancestor of a famous, Scottish family. It then seems to have reverted to the Crown as we find that, in the reign of David II, that monarch granted the barony of Luffness to one Walter Bickerton, in whose family it must have remained for a considerable time. It then passed into the hands of the Hepburns, followed by the Hamiltons, and eventually into the possession of the Hope family, the present proprietors. This family is a branch of the Hopetouns, one of their ancestors being Sir Alex. Hope, K.C.B., one of the Duke of Wellington's Peninsular heroes, and a brother of the good John, Earl of Hopetoun, whose monument crowns the Garleton Hill.

At the time the Bickerton family had possession of Luffness, a chapel stood within the policies, a little to the west of the house, belonging to the Carmelites, or White Friars, some remains of which building are still standing. Within an arched niche of this old chapel lies the statue of a man, life-size, a shield on his breast,

*Bickerton's Tomb*

and a sword grasped in his right hand. This is supposed to be the statue of Friar Bickerton, and locally the spot goes by the name of *"Bickerton's Tomb"*. It often used to be visited by villagers, when the grounds were open on Sunday afternoons. Since the foregoing was written the restoration of this old chapel has been taken in hand with a view to its preservation.

One of the Bickertons attended the Earl of Douglas, as esquire, at the battle of Otterburn, in connection with which tradition tells a very discreditable tale. Otterburn appeals to the young mind as one of the most stirring episodes in Scottish history, when a dead Douglas won the battle. But did the Douglas fall at the hands of his enemies, the English? No, he was stabbed in the back by Lord Bickerton, in revenge for some supposed insult. Presumably it was for this treachery that Lord Bickerton was afterwards outlawed, and eventually slain, not far from his own gates, by a neighbouring baron, Ramsay of Waughton. The spot where the traitor met his death is in the vicinity of Luffness, and goes by the name of *"Bickerton's Gate"*. Such is the story according to tradition, one that cannot now be either corroborated or refuted; but let us hope, for the honour of a Scottish baron, and the good name of Luffness itself, it is not true.

In a green park, which skirts the north side of Luffness gardens may still be traced the outlines of two fish-ponds, used by the monks for the preservation of the piscatorial tiends to which they were entitled from the neighbouring fishermen. In another park, in the opposite direction from Luffness House, there is a tall square building, called the *"Well Tower"*, a name which speaks for itself as to the use for which it was erected. A private avenue runs through this park, which has a sylvan beauty all its own, and there are many other delightful walks in and around the policies, which, unfortunately have, for a long time, been closed to the visitor.

During the wars of the Reformation, Luffness came to be a place of much importance, and it was about this time that the old fortalice was built by the Normans who, with the assistance of their Scottish comrades, long held the place against the Protestant forces. The entrance to this fortalice, remains fairly intact, and abuts on the present public road, being a striking object of interest to the many motorists and others who pass that way, and is locally designated *"The Pend"*. One can see at a glance the immense thickness of the walls forming this portal, or outer entrance, and there is also evidence of a moat having surrounded the stronghold, all going to show how much importance had been placed upon Luffness as a place of defence. On examination of the portal, or Pend, one may recognise the Norman style of masonry, testifying to the skill of those French troops; and further west along the public road the antiquarian will detect more of the same kind of work upon the lintels of the windows of what is now used as a bothy.

When Haddington was garrisoned by the English in the Protestant cause, a strong body of French troops was dispatched to Luffness, in order to intercept the supplies sent by sea to the English garrison. The fortalice of Luffness had a strong position, overlooking the Peffer Burn, and having a wide view of Aberlady Bay, where the ships landed their cargoes for Haddington. Much skirmishing took place, and many lives were lost on both sides. The Catholic troops, however, were unable to achieve their object, except in a partial manner, as the Haddington garrison held out to the end; and the Scottish Reformation became an established fact.

Once the wars of the Reformation ended, the Government decreed that the fortalice of Luffness be destroyed. This was done, but not completely, as it is quite evident that the main portion of Luffness House was built upon the walls of the old fort. The Hepburns built the modern mansion house in 1584, and

General Sir Alex. Hope renovated it around the end of the eighteenth century. It was further renovated and extended by his successors, who, fortunately, were all desirous of preserving the amenities and antiquities thereof. At the entrance to the hall is a massive iron-studded door, a reminder of the warlike times gone by; and the walls of the interior are covered with pikes, and guns, and bows, along with the more modern implements connected with the chase and golf. The last proprietor of this fine old mansion and estate was killed in the Great War, and his son and heir is still a minor.

At the time of the Napoleonic wars Luffness again came into prominence. The Government of the day had a lively dread that the French would invade our shores, and Aberlady Bay was considered one of the most likely places for their landing. Consequently, the authorities once more made Luffness an outpost of defence. A company of militia was stationed here, in order to watch the coast, and give the alarm in case of any attempted landing. Of course the mansion-house, in this instance, was not brought into service, but the men were quartered in huts, etc., put up for the purpose. One of these may still be seen - a red-tiled shed set among a few trees in the park just over the wall at the corner of the road opposite the wooden footbridge that spans the Peffer. Of course, as we all know, the French never landed here or anywhere else, and, perhaps, never had any intention of doing so.

# Kilspindie

HUNDREDS of years before the town and port of Aberlady had become known, or the venerable old church tower had been erected to overlook the waters of the bay, mention is made in ancient historic records of Kilspindie as being a seat of the Culdees. This was one of the earliest Christian sects in the country, and existed somewhere between the seventh and ninth centuries. Not much is known of them, different opinions being held as to the nature of their religious beliefs, but they seem to have dwindled in numbers until they became absorbed by the more powerful monasteries throughout the country, somewhere about 850. The name itself "*Cil-ys-pen-du*", meaning the cell of the black heads, or hoods, bears out the nature of the original building. There is little doubt that at this early date Aberlady Bay presented quite a different appearance to what it does now. The monks or anchorites, of Kilspindie were no doubt sheltered from the west by a fairly large headland covering the rocks that now gird the shore at that point and the bay must have been much deeper, and the shore on this side closer upon the open Firth.

In the reign of David I the lands of Kilspindie were conferred upon the Bishopric of Dunkeld, and remained so until the Reformation. In the warlike and exciting, but likely unhappy and upsetting, days of the various James', Kilspindie came into the hands of perhaps the most renowned family in Scottish history. The famous Bishop Gavin Douglas granted these lands to his equally famous half-brother, Sir Archibald Douglas, designated, after a certain episode, "*Bell-the-Cat*", and in the hands of this great family it must have remained for a considerable time. Patrick Douglas, a grandson of Sir Archibald's, built a fortress at Kilspindie in the year 1585, a year after Luffness House was originally built. This Patrick Douglas of Kilspindie was Treasurer of Scotland during the minority of James V. This old fortress, standing midway between Aberlady village and the shore, has long been in ruins, very little of it being now in existence. What remains there are may be seen in the middle of what is now the Glebe, and this may also be taken as the site of the more ancient "*Cell of the Black Hoods*".

Much of the masonry of the ruined fortress of the Douglas' at Kilspindie (this is the real and genuine Kilspindie) must have been used in the boundary walls afterwards erected in this vicinity, and the same may be said of the old chapel in Luffness grounds, as the observant eye may often detect the old hewn stones in the construction of the surrounding walls. It would be quite an interesting hobby to one of an antiquarian turn of mind to take some time and expend some thought and imagination in an examination of our wayside dykes.

In connection with the old walls that skirt the public road, and the building thereof, a very terse local saying had its origin, and is worth preserving. These were the days of low wages and poor living, when people were glad of a small pittance earned at any kind of work, to keep the needs of the body supplied. It appears that many local men were employed at the building of these dykes, indeed anyone who was at the time out of employment, and was able to put in a day's work, was taken on, and paid at the rate of nine pence per day. The work must have continued for a considerable time, and the men came to look upon it as a sure means of getting a few coppers when in need; so it came to be a saying among them, "Come nicht, come ninepence". Perhaps it is little known and seldom heard now, but the old folks of Aberlady must remember of its often being quoted by their elders, who meant to assume that the end of the day would bring its own reward.

Another local saying, no doubt quite unfamiliar to the rising, and even the passing, generation, was often upon the lips of the villagers in olden times, the origin of which may only be conjectured.

It lacks the epigrammatic pith of the one quoted already, but surely reveals an unusual habit:-

"Guid stick us a', the folk o' Aberlady
Eat the flesh afore the kail is ready."

When this was cast up in derision to old natives it often angered them very much, as reflecting upon their uncivilised manners, but one old dame of spirit is said to have retorted to her tormentors – "Faith, if that's the way o't, ye may stick us a', for we are a' tarr'd wi' the same stick." It will be noticed in the foregoing "saw" the word flesh is used instead of the ordinary beef or meat. The stranger, looking about for something out of the common, will doubtless also notice that the village butcher is called "flesher", and think that the folk of Aberlady have retained some old-fashioned way of their own and don't know any better. Yes, they have a way of their own, but they do know better, for a man may be a flesher - a dealer in flesh or beef - and not a butcher. Many a flourishing merchant in our up-to-date big towns has the designation "butcher" above his premises who is really nothing of the kind.

No son of the village, so far as can be traced, ever attained to world-wide reputation but many did good service to their country in their day. Old Aberlady families, besides those already referred to in these pages, who were widely known for their character or position, or the work they produced, may here be recalled - the Brysons, the Burts, the Dunns, the Frasers, the Eeles, the Lambs, the Mabons, the Mitchells, the Merrilees, the Sinclairs, the Watts, the Walkers, etc. Descendents of many of these may still be found in Aberlady, for it seems to be a characteristic of the place that when a family once settles here it remains until it finally becomes extinct.

# Famous Farmers

EAST LOTHIAN used to be looked upon as "the Garden of Scotland", its fertile and well-farmed fields yielding crops second to none in the country, and some of the best farmers and most highly cultivated fields were to be found in the parish of Aberlady. It is said that the first attempt to cultivate potatoes on anything like an extensive scale in Scotland was done at Craigielaw, when Mr. Hay was tenant, about 1754. Among noted farmers who advanced the science of agriculture in the district may be mentioned the Skirvings of Luffness Mains, the Mylnes of Lochill, the Croils of Spittal, the Reids of Ballencrieff, the Pringles of Ballencrieff Mains, and the Gardiners, afterwards the Puntons, of Aberlady Mains. It is a remarkable fact that in the two neighbouring farms of Lochill and Ballencrieff Mains the families should produce, about the same time, men not only skilled in agriculture, but of decided literary acquirements. James Mylne of Lochill and Andrew Pringle of Ballencrieff both belonged to families who had been life-renters of their respective farms for generations, and both farms were on Lord Elibank's estate. Of their literary work something more is required than a mere passing mention.

James Mylne of Lochill was a poet of no mean order, a volume of his poems and two tragedies being published after his death by William Creech of Edinburgh in 1790. He was a contemporary of Burns, and was overshadowed by the brilliant genius of that poet; otherwise his works might have attained much greater popularity and fame. Like Burns, also, he died young, so that for a time he must have been a prolific writer. His two tragedies were entitled "*British Kings*" and "*Darthula*", each extending to five acts, and might be placed on a level with Home's "*Douglas*" in the manner of which they were planned and written. The scene of "*British Kings*" is laid in the south of England when the Britons and Saxons were at war. I need not seek an excuse for quoting a few passages from Mylne's works to show the high standard to which they attained. One of the characters in the first-named tragedy seemed to be a mediator between the contending parties, and thus addresses them: —

"You see our island in itself is blest with every requisite to man's content; Did nature's God from every other land thus severe it by wide tempestuous seas, and gird it with its rocky walls t'enclose Barbarians who should prey on one another? Were strength and valour given us to defeat the great Creator's blessings? Surely not. But should dissention raise the unnatural rage of mutual slaughter in your valiant breasts, 't would but drive back the weak on their destruction, Hence learn to live in concord, and improve the arts of peace."

His other tragedy, *"Darthula"*, has its scene laid in Ireland, on the coast of Ulster or *"Ullin"*, as the poet calls it. It also deals with warlike times. Darthula is the heroine, and there are some fine passages between her and her lover, Nathos, as, for instance, when she ruminates: —

"Nathos will soon be here. The morning now already blushes o'er us. Yon long streams brighten the tremulous ocean shore where soon the glorious sun shall blaze above the waves."

And she addresses him thus: —

"Young soldier, I disturb your private thoughts. I break, perhaps, some plans of future conquest, or great ideas of expected fame. Such contemplations to the brave, I'm told, afford a joy akin to real victory."

To which Nathos replies: —

"No joy, no pleasure is to me like this with which Darthula's presence fills my breast. Sweet are the hopes of fame! Revenge is sweet for my dear kinsmen slain! But when with thee heedless of fame, unmindful of revenge, a gentler passion gives me sweeter joy! Oh! Could 1 hope that fair Darthula felt with me such pleasure, we should never part; not e'en old age should lessen our delight, but turn youth's raptures to a milder joy!"

Mylne wrote many songs and shorter poems of much merit, also, which all went to show that he was a man of high intellectual attainments and real poetic genius. We are told by the Rev, Dr Carfrae in the preface he wrote to Mylne's book—"His genius led him at an early period of his life to poetry, and his taste in that line of composition was afterwards cultivated and improved by a regular and liberal academical education and an acquaintance with the best ancient and modern poets." Robert Burns and James Mylne, contemporary Scottish poets, were known to each other, and it is interesting to know that the last poem written by the Aberlady poet was a long epistle addressed to Burns, in which he invited the Ayrshire poet to Lochill. A verse or two may be quoted: —

> "I hope ye think na I bespatter ye,
> Like mony mair, wi' fulsome flattery;
> Far less to rouse yer anger's battery
> Was my intent;
> To let ye ken I'd like to clatter wi' ye
> Was a' I meant,
> I seldom cringe to wealth or fame,
> Or o' their freendship coont the name;
> For the maist feck I live at hame,
> A farmer douce,
> Amang my bairnies and their dame
> In this thackt house.

I downa bide to hear a glutton Fraizin'
aboot fine beef an' mutton;
I never ken or care a button
        What I'm to get;
But leave the wife her will to put on
        The pat or spit.
My mind in this yell pairtly see—
Gif ye dislike it, let it be-
But gif it chance to please,
        and ye think it worth whyle,
Eastward frae Edinbro' by the sea
        But fourteen mile.
Ride thro' the toon o' Prestoupans,
Three miles ayont that leave the sands,
Then ither twa thro' guid rich lands,
        You'll find Lochill,
And ready there at your commands
        Yer freend James Mylne."

The two brother farmers and brother poets never met, for, before
Burns found an opportunity of answering this epistle, Mylne had
departed this life.    Shortly afterwards, in the course of a
correspondence with Dr Carfrae anent the publication of Mylne's
verses, Burns wrote: — "I am much to blame; the honour Mr.
Mylne has done me, greatly enhanced in its value by the
endearing, though melancholy, circumstances of its being the last
production of his muse, deserved a better return. I have, as you
hint, thought of sending a copy of this poem to some periodical
publication, but, on second thoughts, I am afraid that, in the
present case, it would be an improper step.    The profits of the
labours of a man of genius are, I hope, as honourable as any
profits whatever, and Mr. Mylne's relations are most justly
entitled to that honest harvest which fate has denied himself to
reap.    But let the friends of Mr. Mylne's fame (among whom I claim
the honour of ranking myself) always keep in eye his respectability as

a man, and as a poet, and take no measure that, before the world knows anything about him, would risk his name and character being classed with the fools of the time."

The volume of Mylne's works was published after his death in 1790, and was subscribed to by almost all the landed proprietors, tenant farmers, clergy, and merchants in East Lothian. It is now very rare, and practically unobtainable, but should any enterprising publisher ever take in hand to produce a new edition, it would be worthy of a wide circulation, and keep alive the fame of a distinguished local genius. James Mylne lies in Aberlady churchyard, side by side with his fathers, and his descendants, his name being simply inscribed upon the family tombstone, without the slightest hint that he was anything else but farmer at Lochhill.

Andrew Pringle of Ballencrieff Mains, although possessed of some literary ability, was a man of quite a different stamp to his neighbour James Mylne. He did not die young by any means, and his inclinations were decidedly more of a practical than a poetic turn. His individuality of character was evinced in many ways that need not here be mentioned. It is related of him that, in his young days, he used to drive cattle from the Highlands to Barnet Fair, near London; a journey of some weeks He was the last of the Pringles of Ballencrieff Mains, who had been tenants there since 1643, and he died somewhere about 1830. Besides being a skilful farmer, he was an extensive grazer in the district, renting Luffness parks among other places.

Andrew Pringle was a man of education, a Latin scholar to boot, and his literary ability was recognised by the Board of Agriculture when they selected him to inspect the rural conditions prevailing in the North of England, and to report thereon. This he did in a treatise entitled *"General View of the Agriculture in Westmoreland"* published in London in 1767. This report was highly esteemed by the Board and the farmers of the time, many expressing themselves very highly as to the quality of the work, both from a practical and literary point of view.

Close beside Ballencrieff Mains, probably part of it at one time, is the site and remains of the Aberlady Brick and Tile Works, an important concern, and the first of its kind in the county. There was a fine bed of clay to draw upon, and bricks, roofing and drain tiles of the best quality were manufactured here. It had only a short life, however, the fact of its being so far from a railway station militating greatly against its chances of success. A square of houses for the workmen stood beside the works, and many stories were told of the wild doings there at one time. Mr. G. Sinclair is now proprietor of the land. One small hut remains which still goes by the name of the Brickwork, and the old clay-hole is gradually being filled and levelled.

## The Story of the Riggs

THE immediate surroundings of Aberlady did not always present the highly cultivated appearance they do now. Previous to the close of the eighteenth century the village lay upon the skirts of a fairly extensive moor, which stretched eastwards far beyond the boundaries of the parish. To the south this moor may have abutted on the lower fields of Ballencrieff Mains farm, and here upon this common the villagers were wont to graze their cattle, horses, etc., for, no doubt, it would afford excellent pasture. It is very probable, also, that some of the villagers would herd their geese here, for a good number of geese used to be kept in the district in olden times. The moor must have been plentifully dotted over with patches of whin bushes, the remnants of which may still be seen - or, at least, were to be seen not so many years ago - in the little wood at the top of the Loan. Perhaps it may be necessary to inform even those who pass it every day that this is the *"Whinny Wud"*. Names such as the *"Muir Road"*, the *"Muir Park"*, etc., still linger to remind us of what these lands were like in the days of our forefathers.

Then, about the end of the eighteenth century a change came over the scene. The big landed proprietors whose estates adjoined this common, and who had, probably, a right to superiority over it, put their heads together, and formulated a plan to have this waste land cultivated. Of course, this could not be done without encroaching upon the grazing rights of the small landlords and feuars of the village, and so the scheme was submitted to them for approval. All appear to have agreed to the proposal except one or two, the most troublesome of whom was a feuar called Black Jock, who strenuously resisted it. This was a check upon the carrying out of the reclamation scheme, and annoyed the promoters. The opposition, however, was in time overcome, although not in a creditable way.

The parish minister of the time, who was, no doubt, a leader in the councils of the landlords and villagers, was induced to play a trick upon the troublesome resister, in order to get him out of the way. Calling upon the unsuspecting Black Jock, he gave him a missive to deliver to a certain party in Leith, who, upon its receipt, saw to it that the bearer was forthwith kidnapped, and kept out of the way for a lengthy period. And so the old moor was divided into lots. The landlord proprietors, of course, got the lion's share, and each of the village feuars got a Scots acre apportioned to them adjoining the south side of the village. Such is the story, traditional, but fairly well authenticated, of the Riggs, the name by which these strips of land became known.

Undoubtedly the old moor is more useful and profitable as it is now; but it can easily be understood that many of the villagers at the time would regret seeing such a drastic change made upon the scene with which they were so familiar. As the years passed on,

Black Jock returned to his native Aberlady, and, before the people knew that he was back among them, he took occasion to call at the Manse, got hold, physically, and unceremoniously, of the minister, and gave him a good ducking in his own well. I have omitted mentioning the minister's name, as it appears that, apart from this discreditable episode, he was a popular and esteemed pastor of the people.

## Golfing Connections

ABERLADY is intimately associated with the origin and development of golf in East Lothian. When the game was first played here no one apparently can tell; or is able to find out, but there must have been a number of golfers in the district in the sixteenth century and onwards. A number of the villagers, and some of the lairds in the district, indulged in the game pretty frequently, held matches, and ultimately combined under the name of the Kilspindie Golf Club. The ground they played on was called the *"Wanster"* course, although there were no artificial made courses then, as we know them now, and it was partly the same as now occupied by the present Kilspindie club.

It was here, also, no doubt, that King James V, the *"Gudeman of Ballengeich"*, came to play golf, when he visited Gosford, as already mentioned. The game must have evoked as much enthusiasm in the old days as it does still, for we are told in the late Rev. John Kerr's *"Golf-book of East Lothian"* that "some natives of Aberlady walked all the way from Glasgow, journeying by night, to enjoy a Handsel Monday game with their friends, and returning the same way." Handsel Monday was a general holiday, and the great gala day of the olden times in East Lothian, and the principal meeting of the year waslong held on that day. But, as time went on, the

Aberlady Company of Volunteers was started, and the late Lord Wemyss, then Lord Elcho, and one of the founders of the Volunteer movement, used his influence in getting a rifle shooting range set out on part of the golf course, and so the old Kilspindie Golf Club was broken up. The Volunteers ousted the golfers at that time, but, as will be seen, the golfers turned the tables on the Volunteers some thirty years later.

The men of Aberlady, so long accustomed to enjoy the royal and ancient game, felt very unhappy in the thought that they had no proper course on which they could play, and again combined to form a club. They approached Mr. Hope of Luffness for use of part of the links on the other side of the bay, were successful in being granted the privilege, and thus the old Luffness Golf Club was formed. The course was laid out by Tom Morris in 1867, and it soon became known as one of the finest courses in the country. Trophies for competition were presented by Lord Elcho (The County Cup), Mr. Hope {The Hope Challenge Medal), and the Rev. J. H. Tait (The Tait Silver Putter), and these are still played for annually.

As the club and course attracted much attention throughout the county, and elsewhere, many golfers from other parts were eager to join, and so Luffness Golf Club increased in importance and popularity. A small clubhouse, rustically built of blue whinstone, and rugged limestone boulders from the seashore, was erected at a convenient spot near the first tee, just beyond "The Timmer Brig" that spans the Peffer Burn. This house may still be seen there, but much enlarged by frequent additions; the original building being of but one modest apartment. There is an illustration of this old clubhouse in the "*Golf-book of East Lothian*", which is of great interest, as a group of the old members are standing on the putting green in front. These include Messrs Frank and Charlie Burnett, the Rev. J. H. Tait, old Mr. McKay, with his "tile" hat on,

*The photograph referred to was not, in fact, found in the publication, though this was.*

John Congalton, Alexander Punton, Robert Tait, Frank Mitchell, James Simpson, and Freddie Dickson. The writer remembers the occasion, for he accompanied his father, who took the photograph, and was also one of the original members of the club. On looking over that group, I find there is not one of them alive to day, and, although their names may be well remembered, they themselves are no more. Such a thing as a bag for carrying the clubs was never thought of in those days, and, indeed, was scarcely necessary, as two or three clubs at the most was all that the players usually carried. Indeed, many capital matches were played, and fine scores recorded by members who went the whole round with nothing more than a trusty cleek.

In a recent article of great interest on East Lothian golf, by W. Whytock, it is truly said that "Luffness Golf Club was a fine example of what a golf club should be. Peer and peasant competed on equal terms, and that grand old man, the late Earl of Wemyss, did all in his power to foster this spirit in our national game." It is related that in May 1875, a match was played at Luffness between the Glasgow Golf Club and Luffness Golf Club, sixteen men aside. It must have been a rather one-sided game, as the Aberlady men, helped by their longer experience, no doubt, won by no less than 92 holes on the two rounds.

In the same year the first regular greenkeeper was appointed, John Anderson, but only on half time, as the conditions were that he "devoted three days a week to the keeping of the green, attend on medal days, and in winter, when no work can be done on the links, to attend at the ice when curling, the salary to be £20 per annum." No work on the links in winter? Why, on a neighbouring course this winter, something like a dozen men might be seen working every day. Old Luffness Golf Club had many members who afterwards made a great name for themselves in golfing circles. For instance, Mr J.E. Laidlaw, the famous amateur, won his first scratch medal here in 1878, and, while the club continued its possession of this course, was very often to be found among the prize-winners. And many local men were not far behind, whose names might be recalled from memory: — Frank Burnett, Alexander Punton, Robert Tait, Tom Harley, the Murrays of the Whim, Harry B. Bryden, etc. The Secretary at that time was John Congalton, widely known in the district, and whose characteristics can never be forgotten by those who knew him. Tom Harley, while yet a young man, emigrated to Canada, and there continued to play golf, winning the championship of that big country on more than one occasion. Other village lads who had learned the game on old Luffness, and have gone to other lands, have helped to foster the love of golf wherever they went, and some who could be mentioned have been in the habit of carrying off the principal prizes in the several districts in which they settled. In the year 1890, or '91, however, at the expiry of the club's lease, the old order of things underwent a change. Mr. Hope of Luffness, proprietor of most of the course, and the Luffness Golf Club had an unfortunate disagreement, with the result that the old club was again to be stranded without the land to play on. So ended another chapter in the history of the golfing pioneers of Aberlady and district. What a loss was theirs! And with what affection must any old members who are left look back upon the bewitching attractions of those rare old links.

Himself a keen member and strong supporter of old Luffness Golf Club, and feeling with other members, the unhappy straits of the situation, Lord Wemyss generously offered ground on the Craigielaw side of the bay for the use of the club. This covered part of what had been the Wanster course, and a few fields were added to make it a full eighteen-hole course. The club gladly accepted the offer, and so changed their headquarters to the land used by the old Kilspindie club, whose name they adopted to suit the change. For some time, the links, especially the fields that were added subsequently, were very rough, but patience and good work gradually brought them back into a satisfactory condition, and now it is one of the finest courses one may wish to see.

For some time after it was opened, members of Kilspindie Golf Club had to cross the rifle shooting range at different points and, when shooting was in progress, a red flag was hoisted in order to warn golfers of the danger of playing certain holes adjacent to the range. This was a most unsatisfactory arrangement for both parties, and eventually the rifle range was closed, and done away with altogether. And so the new Kilspindie Golfers ousted the old Volunteers, just as, a quarter of a century or more earlier, the new Volunteers had ousted the old Kilspindie golfers.

Meanwhile Mr H. W. Hope of Luffness, who was also keen on golf, sought the advice and assistance of old Tom Morris, and forthwith laid out another course on the old links, nearer the Gullane side. A new club was then formed, and took the name of the New Luffness Golf Club. This club acquired on lease the course laid out by Mr. Hope, and proceeded to use and improve upon it. As it is often the experience with a new venture, New Luffness had its own struggles in its initial years, but now it is a most flourishing concern. It is interesting to note that among its original members was that brilliant amateur, Lieutenant Freddy Tait. Among its present members are one or two upon whom Scotland is building some hopes of retaining her reputation in the golfing world.

## General Attractions

LOWLY situated upon the border of its own bay, Aberlady village is well sheltered from the extreme force of the prevailing winds, and, although it is openly exposed to the north, the wind seldom blows from that direction. It is also in one of the driest districts, if not the driest, in Scotland, the average rainfall being about 21 inches per annum. Being in close proximity to the sea, frost is much less keen than in the more inland situations, and snow seldom lies long. Under these conditions, Aberlady is becoming favourably known as a desirable winter residence, as well as a summer holiday resort. Even in the dead of winter, outdoor recreations can generally be pleasantly indulged in. And to certain sportsmen there is the additional attraction of sea fowling, Great numbers, and a great variety, of birds frequent the bay, which is a favourite haunt of the naturalists who wish to study their ways. Some of the migratory birds come to us as summer visitors, but most of them come in the wintertime. Among the latter are large numbers of wild geese, and wild ducks of nearly all the native varieties, as well as occasional specimens of the rarer foreign kinds.

There is much to interest and occupy the time of the geologist in the examination of the various strata of the coast, and the collection of fossils, which may be found in abundance by the seashore. There is also, in the adjacent links, the field-paths, and the woodlands a wide and well stocked field for the study and delight of the botanist. Places of interest to the antiquarian have already been referred to, while, if none of these things appeal to the would-be residenter, well, he can go to the rocks when the tide is flowing into the bay and fish for flounders, and if his fishing operations are unsuccessful, he can pick up among the rocks around him plenty of mussels of the best quality to fill his creel.

At the western extremity of Kilspindie Golf Course, and where the old Volunteer rifle range used to be, is a nice little sandy bay in the making, which one of our visitors some years ago dubbed "*Shell Bay*", a name which is pretty generally applied to it now. It is easily understood how it got its name, for along the high-water mark there is a great profusion and endless variety of beautiful little shells. What a delight the gathering of these shells is to the children fortunate enough to be squatted here in the long hours of a summer day. Even those of mature years are sometimes tempted to indulge in the same delightful occupation, examining and classifying the specimens found, and lost in wonder, it may be, at the beauty of the little things often trod underfoot. The majority of these shells belong to a bygone age, when all this low lying land was under the sea, for no live specimens of many of these varieties are to be found in the district now. They have been washed out of the sand-dunes by the inroads of the sea, the "bones", I might say, of the shellfish which abounded here many hundreds of years ago. The proper name of this spot is *"Green Craig"*, which was at one time a green promontory jutting out into the sea. The little island facing *"Shell Bay"*, which one sees when the tide is full, represents about all that is left of the original green craig. It is here that the ever-increasing inroads of the sea are most apparent. Our fathers would scarcely recognize the place were they to return and see it now. Even those of the present generation must observe the difference it presents in appearance.

A very good example of the changing coastline may be found in the fact that one of the butts of the Volunteer shooting range, a substantial piece of masonry, which was, when is use, a good many yards in from the shore, is now as many yards under the high-water mark, and a mere heap of stones. Upon the coastline from this point to the public road, which is the north-western boundary of the parish, the sea is working serious damage. A well-built bulwark faced the sea along this part in our early days, but it is now seriously eaten into, very little of it remaining intact. When a west gale accompanies a high tide, as it often does, the waves dash themselves furiously against this obstruction, tear down the bulwark that was so carefully erected to keep them at bay, and toss about its solid masonry as if it were so many chuckie-stanes. It is interesting to speculate on what may be the reason for all this change. Why should the sea be swallowing up considerable parts of the coast here, while on the other side of the bay, the Gullane side, the land is gradually working itself into the sea? Can it be that the direction or force of the prevailing winds has changed in modern times? That may be so to a certain extent, but it cannot in itself account for the change. The real and principal cause is more likely to be this. Compared with even fifty years ago, a much larger and higher bar of sand stretches away westward from Jova's Neuk to a point nearly opposite Kilspindie. This bar materially protects the upper, or eastern, part of the bay from the stormy seas, and effectually breaks the force of the waves long before they reach the shore on the Gullane side. The bay itself has been gradually, sometimes indeed rapidly, filling up with sand, until now it is smaller as well as much shallower than it used to be. Now, as is well known, water must always find its own level, and as the bay cannot now contain the quantity it used to do, that immense volume of water must find its level, or, in other words, a bed for itself elsewhere. Naturally it will flow in upon the nearest opening it can find, and the vicinity of Green Craig answering to this, and being at the same time exposed to the western gales, it is here that the sea is, of necessity, struggling to find for itself a resting place.

To the ever-increasing number of visitors to Aberlady, diversified as their tastes will undoubtedly be, there is no mistake that golf is now, and likely to remain, the chief attraction. The golf courses in the immediate vicinity have already been described and their history recalled. New Luffness and Kilspindie - the latter having a very successful ladies section - are within easy reach of the village, and each of them has charms of its own. A little further afield, but still within three miles, are the fine old courses of Gullane to the east, and the highly attractive course of Longniddry to the west. To those whose inclination lies more in the direction of bowling, their taste can be provided for at the bowling green already mentioned at the west end of the village.

This is one of the best greens in East Lothian, a county famed for its many fine bowling greens. Here the game can be had at a moderate expense, whether the visitor desires to become an ordinary member or a monthly member. A comfortable pavilion has recently been erected, where players can shelter or rest if need be. Then, what may appeal more to the majority of young ladies who come to the village, a tennis court was recently laid out near the old Luffness club house, an easy and pleasant ten minutes walk away. It is a grass court, but of fine quality of turf, and at present there is an intention of having it extended. Here again the charge is very moderate.

In the summer months motor char-a-bancs make periodic excursions into the surrounding countryside, affording an opportunity of seeing many places of interest and beauty. It may be said that there is no fine stretch of sands nearby for the delectation of the children. That, unfortunately, is true, but there are the fairly extensive Eastern and Western Sea-Greens, where children can play in safety among the knowes and howes, roll about over the soft green turf to their heart's delight, and gather for themselves posies of wildflowers to their abounding wonder and delight. Is there anything in life half so sweet, half so satisfying and comforting to the soul, as to see with the eyes of a child the marvelous revelation and surprising beauty of an opening flower ?

Surely enough has been said regarding the many-sided attractions of Aberlady as a holiday resort, to satisfy and convince the stranger that it is quite a desirable place in which to live. An English gentleman, with a business connection in Edinburgh, and a holiday acquaintance with the village once declared to the writer – "If a person once takes up his residence in Aberlady, there is to him for ever thereafter only one place in the world he calls his home.". I was struck, at the time, with the convincing tone of his declaration, and from personal observation since, I have frequently seen it illustrated. As has already been said, however, the accommodation is limited, but the greater the demand, the greater will be the chances of its being increased. We have, in the summer months at least, a good service of trains, and, with a larger population, the winter service might be improved.

Aberlady was one of the first villages in Scotland to introduce gas-lighting, and electric power is gradually coming nearer. Our water supply is ample, and of good quality, and most of the houses have now the usual modern conveniences, so that none of the disabilities of many country places need frighten the intending visitor, who may be struck with the picturesqueness of the village, and the rural beauties of its surroundings, from taking up his abode here.

It was supposed that the enquiring stranger had come to Aberlady from the west, entering the parish at the open, breezy, and romantic corner of Boglehill, and having paid his visits to the various places of interest within our bounds, he will pursue his way eastward, and leave the precincts of the parish at another beauty spot, Luffness Mill. Here the road takes a sharp turn northwards to the Gullane Links, and no one who can take time to have a look about him can fail to appreciate the sylvan beauty of the immediate surroundings. Just before he turned his back upon it, he would notice the deeply shaded Long Avenue stretching away to Luffness Mains in the distance, and just before him he will doubtless be struck with the picturesque buildings of the old water-mill.

*Luffness Mill*

All lovers of the beautiful touches in our rural scenery must feel a debt of gratitude to the proprietors of this old mill for keeping the original quaintness of its features in good repair. Especially in autumn does the striking beauty of this corner arrest the observant eye—the old rustic gateway, with the green ivy clinging around its base, the rich deep brown of the beeches, the sombre green of an occasional pine, with the grey-sage coloured foliage of the drooping willows, the soft gurgle of the little burn that ripples along under the roadway, and the happy "twick-twick" of some harmless waterfowl, as they feed along its brim, all combine to make the impression sink deep into the memory.

The attention of the reader of this "Guide to Aberlady" has been called to places of interest strictly within the limits of the parish but all round about the county there are scenes of historic fame, well-known places of beauty, and even wider facilities for the game of golf, and all who may have any of these objects in mind, could not find a more desirable centre from which to make their excursions than the village of Aberlady.

# EELES

## Butchers & Poulterers

# ABERLADY
# & GULLANE

ESTABLISHED 1790

ABERLADY—Phone No. 4.
GULLANE—Phone No. 5.

# Furnished Houses and Apartments.

SITTING-ROOM, 2 Bedrooms, with Attendance. Mrs BORTHWICK, Winton Place.

SITTING-ROOM, 2 Bedrooms, with or without Attendance. Mrs Gow, Bayview.

BED-SITTING-ROOM, and Bedroom, 2 beds, with Attendance. Miss MILLER, The Cairn.

APARTMENTS.—2 Bedrooms, with Attendance. Mrs CRAWFORD, Bickerton Place.

SPRINGLEA.—Sitting Room, 3 Bedrooms, use of Kitchen, Bathroom, etc. Mrs THOMSON.

MERRILEES COTTAGE.—Sitting Room, Bedroom, Kitchen, Scullery, etc. Mrs LAMBERT.

ROSE COTTAGE.—Sitting Room, 2 Bedrooms, (3 Beds), Bathroom, etc. Mrs W. GUY.

SITTING-ROOM, 2 Bedrooms, Bathroom, etc., with Attendance. Mrs STRACHAN, Manor Place.

SITTING-ROOM, 2 Bedrooms, Bath, (H. and C.), with Attendance. Mrs AITKEN, Laurieville, Pleasance.

SITTING-ROOM, 2 Bedrooms Bathroom, etc. with, or without Attendance. Mrs MARTIN, Pleasance.

BED-SITTING-ROOM, and Bedroom, (2 Beds), Kitchen, Bath, etc. Mrs JOHNSTONE, Pleasance.

# Furnished Houses and Apartments.

ELLEN VILLA.—Public Room, 2 Bedrooms (3 Beds), Bathroom, &c. Mrs Boyd.

HALL HOUSE.—Sitting Room, 4 Bedrooms (3 Beds), Kitchen and Conveniences. Also Cottage, 2 Rooms, all Conveniences. Mrs Rutherford.

SITTING-ROOM, 2 Bedrooms, Bathroom, &c. With or without Attendance. Mrs Taylor, Hope Terrace.

SUNNYBRAE.—Parlour, 4 Bedrooms, Kitchen, Bathroom, &c. Rain.

SITTING-ROOM, Kitchen, 3 Bedrooms, &c. Mrs Stewart, The Gardens, Aberludy.

LOAN VILLA.—Sitting Room, 3 Bedrooms, Kitchen, &c. Mrs Sinclair.

SITTING-ROOM, Bedroom, Bath, &c. Mrs Wells, 11 Pleasance.

APARTMENTS.—Good Rooms and Fine Situation. Mrs Stark, Main Street, Aberludy.

SITTING-ROOM and Bedroom, with Attendance. Miss Dunn, "The Cottage," Aberludy.

SITTING-ROOM and Bedroom, with Attendance. Mrs C. Fortune, Poplar Cottage, Aberludy.

# *SPORTS.*

## *ABERLADY TENNIS CLUB.*

Two Grass Courts at Old Luffness Golf Club House.

Miss A. Glasgow, Secretary and Treasurer,
Luffness Club House.

## *ABERLADY BOWLING CLUB.*

Good Green and Convenient Club-house.

### *Membership Fee—7s. 6d.*

G. Fortune, Secretary and Treasurer.

## *KILSPINDIE GOLF CLUB.*

A Favourite East Lothian Course.
Commodious and Well-appointed Club-house.

J. Bowie, Secretary and Treasurer.

## *ABERLADY MINIATURE RIFLE CLUB.*

Capital Range at Drill Hall,
—Open Winter Evenings. —

### *Entry Fee and Subscription—3s. 6d.*

Jas. Gow, Secretary and Treasurer.

"It seems to be a characteristic of the place that, when a family once settles here, it remains until it finally becomes extinct."

J. P. Reid

Aberlady is very fortunate to benefit from the writings of John Pringle Reid (1862-1930). Most of what he wrote concerned the village, its parish, its environment and its people.

This particular work deserves special appreciation. Although there are other historical accounts of Aberlady's past, none possess that characteristically flowing narrative of Reid, who lifts our history from the preserve of the dry antiquarian to charm both villagers and visitors alike.

The book brings to mind an earlier time when the pace of life was slower but no less rich and perhaps more rewarding. A few new photographs and other relevancies have been added in this second edition.

**Acknowledgements**
We gratefully acknowledge the support of the Heritage Lottery Fund (through the Awards for All programme), East Lothian Council, the Strathmartine Trust and Gullane Area Community Council in the publication of this work.

*Aberlady Conservation Society 2006*

*£8.99*